AF255811

My Superman
Has Left the Building

My Superman Has Left the Building

Dealing with the Loss of Losing My Father,
Donnie D. Williams

By AVA MONTGOMERY

RESOURCE *Publications* · Eugene, Oregon

I dedicate this book to my father, Donnie Williams. He was my first love and my best friend. He was my angel sent in human form to protect, love, and care for me. To a man that who showed me how to become an outstanding individual by leading by example. To the man that who showed me that it was important to care for others as I cared for myself. I never had to look for anyone to look up to because I lived in the house with a hero I respected and loved and admire to this very day. I dedicate this book to every person out there who has lost their beloved father and would give anything to see and touch him again. This book is dedicated to a person that woke up the morning after losing their father and felt like you were in a dream. This book is dedicated to every person who has had to feel the pain that cannot be described only felt when the man that was your first role model, first admirer, first support, and superman was removed from your life and you had to wake up every day to find the strength to go on.

This book is dedicated to the many women and men just like me who deal with waking up every morning knowing you will never see your father's face on this side again . . .

Contents

Preface

I will never forget the day that I received the phone call, and they told me that you were gone, the pain that I felt that day I cannot describe. There are no words to tell you about the numbness that was in my heart or the pain that has never left since that day. The pain of losing a father can only be felt and never imagined, the pain of getting up and going on with you not being present in my life is so unbearable that all I can say is, "Lord Help Me Please." The pain of losing my father has kept me awake many days, crying, going to bed, and crying to just get out of my bed. Words cannot begin to tell you how this hurts. I don't think that mere words could ever touch on that. I would give anything to see him one more time. I would give anything to hear him call my name and tell me what I am doing wrong and how to fix it. I just wish that I could hold his hand and tell him that I am doing better and how much I love him for always being there. My daddy, my sweet daddy, God got the best man I have ever known. People say that life goes on but to me that is the saddest part. I must get up broken-hearted and know that I'll never see you on this side again and that knocks the wind out of me every day.

Acknowledgments

I want to thank God and my children. I want to send a special thank you to my siblings, mom, and family.

Lastly to all of my readers that have gone out and supported me since my first book, thank you, thank you, thank you so much for believing and investing in my dreams, I am thankful for each and every one of you. My story, his glory!

This Cannot Be Real

It seems so unreal. I hear everyone tell me that you have passed away but for some reason that is not registering to me. How could there be a day when I can't see your face and hold your hand? How could there be a day when you would leave me? Daddy, I can't believe that you are gone. I loved you so much, and now today as I stand, a part of my heart feels like it has died 50 times over and again and again. I am so broken, and I am so lost for words. My daddy is gone. I would give anything to hear my daddy call my name one more time. I would give anything to hear him say baby its ok. I would give anything daddy to have you back. I am so angry I feel like out of all the people that are out here in this world, why did God have to take you? My daddy? Lord I just need another day with my daddy. I need your advice; I need your hug and I need your smile. I need you daddy and I need you back badly. I am so hurt daddy that I cannot see the days or weeks without you. Daddy, how do I go on? How do I live knowing I will never see you again. I will never get to watch a movie or invite you over for dinner. You won't be there the day I get married to walk me down the aisle and see the kids graduate. Daddy, Oh how I need you? Daddy, I am not that strong. Daddy, I can't do this without you. Daddy, please come back to me. I feel like I am so numb, I look at your car and I still cannot believe that you have left me. I need you so bad daddy. What do I do now? Who am I going to call? Who do I turn to? Daddy Please I am so devastated My whole world feels like it is over. I miss you so much daddy. I just want to tell you I heard you. I listened to the lessons that you taught me. Daddy, if you come back, I will get it right this time. Daddy, I miss you so much. oh, daddy my heart is breaking. I feel so lost without you in my life. Daddy, I wish I could see him one more time. I would like to spend the whole day with you.

God Needed a Superman

God needed a Superman.
to help him out up above
He wasn't looking for just a regular man.
but he needed one that was dearly loved.

God needed a Superman.
that loved helping people everyday
God needed a Superman.
that would help people find their way.

God needed a Superman.
then he looked down and saw you
He watched your acts of kindness.
and assigned work in Heaven, only you could do

God needed a Superman.
and he said Donnie, it's time to come home
Then Donnie asked, "What about my family?"
I don't want to leave them alone.

God said, "I will take care of them.
But son you have to come along."
God opened the gates of Heaven.
and said, "Donnie here is where you belong".

God Said, " First you were my Superman.
And I gave you to your family for a while
Here you will praise and have joy
And always walk around with a smile".

You see God needed a Superman
and he needed a very special man.
So, God sent for our daddy.
to complete his perfect plan

God needed Donnie, Our Superman
and today in peace he now stands.
I see him walking around Heaven so happy.
with Earlie Mae, and Jesus hand in hand.

To Tell You

To tell you that I miss you.
would not be enough.
to tell you that I'm still going.
when it is tough

To Tell you that I am living.
and that everything is ok
To tell you all that would be a lie daddy
Because I cry for you everyday

To Tell you that I understand
when inside it hurts so much
to tell you that it is getting better.
when your hand I wish I could touch

To tell you that I am happy.
right now, I cannot say.
I cry every night I go to bed
and mourn for you everyday

To tell you that the pain gets better
when I do not think that it will
The pain that I am enduring.
you cannot imagine you have to feel

To tell you that I've accepted
that I cannot call you anymore
You see that I haven't dealt with
Because I'm still waiting for you to walk through the door

I Can't

I can't accept the fact.
that you are gone away
I can't accept the fact that I can't call you
Just to say Hey

I can't accept the fact.
that I can't call you when somethings wrong
I can't accept the fact.
that when you did you were all along

I can't accept the fact.
that I can't see you anymore
I can't accept the fact that when I go to your house
You're not waiting for me by the door.

I can't accept the fact.
that I cannot see your face
but I do believe Daddy.
That you are in a better place

I cannot accept the fact
that right by your side I can't be.
but I have accepted the fact that.
You have no worries and now you are free.

Everyday

Every day I wake up
and it's like I had a nightmare.
when I wake up in the mornings
I feel like my life is not fair.

Every day I look to the sky
and wonder how you are.
Somedays I feel so close to you.
and other days you seem so far.

Every day I wish I could see you
just for a minute or two
Every day I cry over you.
and causes pain I never knew

Every day I think about you.
and the things you said to me.
Every day I hear you say Keep Going
I'm happy as can be.

Every day I smile daddy.
or at least I pretend.
Every day I wake up crying.
because I have lost my best friend

My World

My world is devastated.
ever since that night
I try not to cry.
I try to act like I am alright.
My world will never be the same.
I look at the phone.
and I can't erase your name

My world is shattering.
When I wake everyday
You left before I was ready.
and there were things I needed to say.
My world feels so empty.
since that day I laid you to rest
I tell everyone I'm fine.
but I am so broken I must confess.

My world feels like it's over
no matter what I do
I'll never get to talk to you
and that makes my whole world blue.

You Taught Me

You taught me to Trust Jesus
and never question his will.
But losing you was so hard.
and accepting it has been a tough pill.
You taught me that God is good.
and that God always knows was best.
But why did God take you.
This has been my hardest test.
You taught me to never give up.
No matter what I face.
But Daddy you were my strength.
When I needed help to run this race
You taught me too always be nice.
You said baby you always be kind
Since the day I buried you
it seems like no peace can I find.
You taught me that life has lessons.
and you taught me right from wrong.
You used to push me to keep going
and now I feel I can't go on.
You taught me so many things.
and now I ask Jesus to help me to
You taught me how to live this life.
But you never taught me how to live without you.

Daddy's Gone

The day that I received the phone call that you were gone I dropped to the floor in disbelief, just as I am today. My father always instilled in me endurance to face life. He was determined that we would overcome whatever problem or obstacle was presented to me. He told me that life will not always be fair and to make the best life possible for my family every day. Many days I wanted to quit but thinking of how hard my father worked for us to become successful, I just keep pressing. Daddy instilled in me so many things. I can name a million-character traits that you instilled in me but now I am facing a losing battle, and Daddy I am losing. My world feels like a nightmare and my heart is barely beating. My life will never be the same. I have changed. To be honest daddy, I hurt day in and out. I made so many mistakes, yet you loved me in spite of them. I wasn't perfect but you treated me as I was. You were my for sure thing. You were the concrete under my feet. I could always depend on you. I knew you would always be there; Boy was I so wrong. I try to go back in my mind and ask myself, "did you know I loved you." I ask myself, "did I show you how much I loved you before you left?" I just want to make sure you know that I really did love you and appreciate you for everything. Daddy, I am so hurt. I never thought that I'd experience this kind of loss in my life. There are so many questions that I want to ask. I get angry at God because sometimes I don't understand why he just couldn't let you stay with me. I wasn't ready for you to go. I wonder how you are doing. I wonder what you are doing. Daddy, I miss you so much till it hurts my soul.

I remember the talks you and I had. I remember how you were my voice of reason when I didn't have one. You were the inner voice that spoke to me all the time to remind me to stay on the right path. Your thoughts and opinions meant the world to me. I feel like I let you down. Daddy, I am so sorry. I asked you to go to the doctor, but you refused and said baby I am fine. I am thinking about the talk we had before you left. You used to tell me that if its God's will, you would be ok with it. You used to say I'll see you tomorrow if its gods will, you willingly accepted gods will no matter what the outcome was. I honestly admit I have tried to be like you, but I can't. God's decision this time is hard for me to accept.

I prayed and asked God to let you live long enough to see all your grandkids become grown. I asked God to let you see me become successful and I felt like God let me down this time. I remember the day I sat in the house, and it was just me and Jesus alone

He reminded me that to be absent from the body is to present with the lord. I asked God to let you stay with me. I told God that he didn't answer my prayer. God said you don't know what your daddy's prayer was to me.

I remember you said you just wanted to live long enough to see all of your children grown and being able to live on. God answered that prayer for you, but I miss you.

There are no words to tell you how much I miss you and how hurt I am. I hurt because I can't see you, talk to you, call you, or hug you. One thing you always told me was that God never makes mistakes. No matter how painful it may seem. Everything works out for your good and that there is always a purpose for your pain.

Why God

God, you promised you love me
and you would always be there.
But I'm angry because.
I feel like taking my dad wasn't fair.

He said daughter don't be mad.
You see, one day I made the world.
I gave you 61 years with your daddy.
and you always be his girl.

I said God I miss my daddy.
Why did you take him from me?
Your father's work on earth was done.
There was somewhere else I needed him to be.

He said you see this life is not promised.
You are only passing through.
Your dad and I discussed things.
about which you never knew

Your father was tired.
and it was time for him to rest.
I know he wasn't ready to leave you.
and it would cause you much distress.

But you see my plan is bigger.
much bigger than you can see.
I let him be with you for 38 years
Now my daughter, I really need him with me.

You see you thought he never knew.
how much you loved him so
but when he realized he had to leave you
it broke his heart for him to go.

He asked me can he still watch over you.
each and every day
The red birds are an indication.
that your father is not that far away

Just yesterday he told me.
to tell you that he is alright.
He doesn't need a drugs or medicine.
and he is happy both day and night.

He said to tell you He's proud of you.
No prouder could he have been.
He said he was happy to see kam graduate
and he saw you in Houston when Javin turned 10.
Your daddy said to tell you.
that he is in a much better place.
It hurts him to see you sad.
and to wipe these tears from your face

You see to absent from the body.
Child, that means your father is with me.
He is smiling happily, and at peace.
and now he is so free

You cannot see it now.
and my ways you don't understand
Just know I'm God, the creator
and I have your life in my hands.

Sometimes

I play your voice message
each and every day
I repeat it daily.
to be near you in some way

I can't explain it sometimes
but I hear your voice in my head
Then I act strong during the day
and I cry while lying in my bed

I call uncle nun sometimes.
and I check on him too.
I call and check on mama
the same things you used to do.

I go to Vivian sometimes.
but I don't stay long.
I expect you to come down the road
then it hits me that you are gone

No matter how many days go.
I'll never get over losing you.
People say I look happy sometimes.
and inside I am broken into.

Dear Daddy, It's Tough

Yesterday I saw you.
make sure we always had enough.
Now I wake up every day.
crying while looking at all your stuff

Too tough to live without you
and I can't hear your voice.
I made decisions and you are not here.
to say I've made a good choice.

It's tough to accept that I must live
and I cannot see your face.
It's tough especially when I drive to Vivian.
And your clothes are all over the place.

It's tough when I think about getting married.
and you will not be there.
It hurts so much.
because I feel like life it's not fair

Its tough lords know it is.
to live each and every day without you
but I keep going because
That's what you would want me to do.

I'm Getting Married Daddy,

I got up this morning
I'm getting Married today.
But all I can do is cry
and in the bed, I want to lay.

I have a dress that is so lovely
and the venue is amazing too.
There only one thing is missing.
And daddy it's you.
My make up will be flawless
and my hair will look nice too.
but I'm getting ready to walk down the aisle
and it is tearing my heart in two.

As I put the wedding dress on
My heart is hurting so bad.
This day is supposed to be joyful.
but this day feels really sad.

I'm going to walk down the aisle.
but it will not be with you.
I have to pretend and wear a smile.
and hold in pain like you never knew.

As I begin to walk down the aisle
tears fell from my eyes.
and no matter how beautiful my wedding is.
All I want to do is cry.

You won't to be here to see me.
Marry the man that I love so
And I can't hold your hand
and ask you daddy, is it ok to let go?

My make up is all messed up.
My dress is white as can be.
I just wish you could be here.
and have a dance with me.

I say my vows to my husband.
and I smile as hard as I can.
then I start to cry really hard
as I look for you in the stand

My husband says its ok
Your daddy is here you know.
As long as you know he loves you.
as he's with you everywhere you go

As he holds my hands
and together we now stand.
I'll love him forever
But you will always be my first man

The Day I Buried my Daddy

Il never forget the day that I buried my father. The memories of that day keep me up at night. All I remember the whole time it was going on was feeling like I was in a nightmare, and I could not wake up from it. I remember looking out into the air and looking for a sign that what my family told me was wrong. I remember the week of the funeral; I stayed outside for hours waiting for my father to pull up and he never did. I remember my sister calling me to tell me that they were going to meet at the funeral home and asking me did I wanted to attend, I remember telling my family that I was in no condition to help plan this ordeal. I felt like I was dying, and I just wanted to see my dad. I called his phone over 40 times waiting on him to pick up and he never did, I could not believe that I was going to a church to bury my irreplaceable father. I never got up to go and the whole time I couldn't get myself together. No matter what I did, I could not mentally prepare myself for that day. I sat in the couch the night before just angry; I remember saying God you could have taken anybody, but you had to take my father. Why? Did God answer? No. If he had it still would not have helped me in the state that I in. I was a mess, and I felt as like my life was over and I believed that it was.

My Dad

My dad was a man.
That always stood tall.
My dad was a man.
That never let me fall.

My dad was a man.
That always had my back.
My dad was a person.
That never let me lack.

My dad was my provider.
When I couldn't take care of myself
My dad was there for me.
When my kids' dads left

My dad was there.
No matter what time I call
My dad pulled me out.
When my back was against the wall

My dad was God's angel.
That he sent to take care of me
My dad told me to hold on and keep going.
And I could be anything I wanted to be.

My dad is remarkable.
And I'm the apple of his eye.
My daddy means so much to me.
When I think about it, I want to cry

My dad's name is Donnie Williams
He's the best man I've ever known
My dad raised me to be successful.
And he showed me how to stand on my own.

My Superman

My Superman didn't have a cape.
And he couldn't fly in the air.
My superman couldn't jump from buildings.
He had to use the stairs

My superman couldn't blow out fires.
And he couldn't go around the world.
My superman doesn't have X-Ray beams.
But he always protected his little girls.

My superman didn't get to earth on a ship.
And he didn't not have an Aunt Mae or Uncle Ben
My superman was a regular man.
That liked to watch movies in the living room den.

My superman didn't make arch enemies.
And you couldn't watch him on TV.
My superman didn't make movies.
And he used prescription eyeglasses to see.

My superman did not have superpowers.
And a custom he did not wear.
My superman couldn't move faster than lightning.
But when I called him, he was always there

My superman was not from Krypton.
And his real name was not Clark Kent
My superman didn't have superpowers.
But he always participated in all my kids' events.

My superman wasn't born galaxies away.
And his eyes did not glow.
My superman is my hero and my father.
He's the greatest superman I will ever know.

Thank You, Daddy, for Loving Me

My dad was my instructor, professor, my friend, my preacher, and my policeman. My dad's name is Donnie Williams. My dad was born and raised in Rodessa, Louisiana. My parents met while they were in high school and married shortly after graduation. My dad was a great father to my siblings and me. My dad was an extremely strict and honorable man. I remember when I was little, my dad worked two jobs and put us in our own home. My dad always taught us to be respectful. My dad gave us the best of everything. My daddy was always there to provide for us. He never walked away from responsibility. He took care of me my whole life. My dad always took us to church when we were little. My father was a deacon at Greater Mt. Nebo Baptist Church. My daddy used to make us go to church every Sunday and attend the prayer meeting thereafter. My daddy always made sure we understood who God was and why we needed to know who he was. My dad told us daily of God's love for us. My dad was such an impressive man. I could use all the words I know to describe him, but even Webster does not contain words that would even come close enough to tell you what this man was to me. The words in the dictionary would not even compare. My dad's love for me was unconditional.

My dad always stood his ground with us even if later he cried about it. My dad's favorite line to me was keep living no matter how hard times got for me. My life didn't go as me, and my family and I planned. My life was spinning out of control. The things that daddy was trying to teach me sounded like a foreign language. The advice he gave me was easily given, but it broke my heart to accept some of the things that he said. Why, Daddy? Because I was young and at one point in my life. I was young, and I thought I knew it all, but later as I have grown older, I realized I was so dumb. That's why Daddy used to say keep living because, you see now that I am older, I understand life is a lesson. If you keep living, life will bring you to your knees. The hard and rough times reminded me of what daddy used to say to me. and All of a sudden, daddy's lessons and advice made so much sense.

Daddy was wise even though I didn't know it back then. Daddy has already been down the road I was traveling on, and he didn't want me to make mistakes that I would later regret. You see, I wasn't a rebellious child, but I was just trying to find out what was this life stuff all about. I was trying to make my mark. My daddy used to tell me tough love was real love. Tough love was real love. My daddy really loved me. I thought my father was just being a mean parent, but he was just practicing tough love. I used to think that he didn't want me to grow up.

My daddy used to tell me that I could not go with my friends.

I couldn't go over my friend's house and spend the night "without me or your mom talking with their parents first."

"You can't stay out past ten."

"You can't watch TV on school nights."

"You can't wear those skirts that short."

"You can't wear that blouse. It's too tight."

"You can't wear lipstick."

"You can't have a boyfriend."

"You can't get in trouble at school."

"You have to complete your chore before going to bed."

My daddy had so many rules. Why, Daddy? Why? All my friends can go. All my friends have them. But my daddy was never intimated. He just looked at me and spoke. "I already told you no, and in my house talking back was never permitted." Every day, it was another lesson. I used to use to say I had the meanest dad in the whole world, but that was when I was a teenager.

Thinking about everything I cry. If I could go back in time, I would sit on my daddy's leg and listen to every word he would say. I would pay attention, and I wouldn't get mad when he said no.

I'm 45 years old now with a 17, 18, and 25-year-old son that asks me the same question that I used to ask my daddy. It was so amazing that yesterday he told me that I was a mean mother. I smiled and wished I could call my wonderful, amazing, wise, and honorable father and say,

Thank you, Daddy, for Saying No.

Thanks, Daddy for not letting me go.

Thanks, Daddy, for grounding me when I disobeyed.

Thank you, Daddy. Now I know why.

You were only doing what was best for me and for that I owe you, my life. Thank you, Daddy. Your NO's saved me and have given me a better life. and now I'm that same mean mother to my kids, and I owe all that I am to you.

Daddy, Why?

Daddy why do we have to wash dishes
We just got out of school.
Daddy why do we have to clean up
While my friends get to go to the pool?

Daddy why do we have to help with laundry
When we want to go outside and play
Daddy why do we have to go to church
It seems like every day.

Daddy why do you deny me.
And you always tell me no.
Daddy, my friend's parents let them.
So, daddy why do you want to let me go?

Daddy why when I leave home.
You say you better be home by ten.
Daddy, why when I go over to a friend's house?
You always tell me to check in.

Daddy why do I have a curfew?
I'm eighteen and I'm grown.
Daddy, you see I have a job
But you say, "You don't have a home."

Daddy because can't I?
I smile as I remember those days.
Daddy thank you for saying NO.
I'm more thankful than words can say.

If I Could Do It All Over Again

If I could do it all over again
I would listen to every word you say.
If I could do it all over again
Dad, I would hug you every day

If I could do it all over again
I would do it so differently this time.
If I could do it all over again
When you say no instead getting upset I would be fine

If I could do it all over again
I would listen and say, "Daddy, you are right."
If I could do it all over again
I'd never go to bed mad at you a night.

If I could do it all over again
I'd tell you; you were much wiser than me
If I could do it all over again
I knew now you saw things I couldn't see.

If I could do it all over again
I'd do it so different you know
Dad you were only protecting me from pain
But the road I traveled caused me to grow

If I could do it all over again
To be honest, Daddy, I wouldn't you see.
Because I'd do it all over but make different choices
As long as my boys are still with me.

21

My Role Model

My daddy is my role model. My daddy has always been the first man I ever looked up to. I remember being little, and my daddy used to work hard all day and come home. After he would eat dinner, he would always spend time with us. My parents would always spend time with us. I remember playing Monopoly on many nights. My siblings and I used to get mad, and sometimes we even cried when we lost, but we had a blast. My daddy taught us that at some point in our life, we would have to experience loss. He said that there will be days when you will have to endure all types of things, but you cannot lose heart. Life is hard. Life is not fair, and complaining about it will not help. Sometimes you will have to accept things in your life and move on. My dad used to say jobs aren't fun, but they are an income for you to be able to take care of your family. My dad used to say, "Always takes care of your family and make sure they always have what they need." My dad said that you must work for everything in your life; nothing was freely given. My dad said that always is a person of character and respect others and you would yourself. He taught me that I should never be afraid to fail. He said that even though falling may hurt, I should just dust myself off and get back up. He said that God would always be there to help me through anything that I would encounter. My daddy did not have a lot of money, but my siblings and I never cared. My daddy loved us, and he never gave up on me. He was my hope on so many days when I felt like I was at my worst. My daddy always accepted me and loved me no matter what. A man that I admire and respect. He is a man that showed me how to become a respectful individual and to never give up on my dreams. A man that shaped four children into hardworking and honest adults. He was the best role model anyone could have.

Thanks Daddy

Thanks, Daddy, for your rules.
And for being so mean
Thanks, Daddy, for the standards.
That the rooms you made us clean

Thanks, Daddy, for your faithfulness.
And taking care of our home
Thanks, daddy, for not leaving mama.
So, she didn't have to raise us on her own.

Thanks, Daddy, for the moments
That was between you and me.
Thanks, Daddy, for allowing me to make choices
That later on caused me to cry.

Thanks, you Daddy for demanding
That we always show others respect
Thank you, daddy, for loving us!
And none of us did you ever neglect.

Thank you, Daddy.
For helping me anytime
Thank you for raising me to be honest
And not get involved into a life of crime

Thank you for being my daddy.
My instructor, professor, and friend
Thank you for loving me Daddy
One of the best things in life god did send

You See

You see when I was young.
I thought I knew it all.
The older I become.
I realize I was clueless to it all.

You see when I was young.
I thought I was so smart.
I thought my parents were just being mean.
And they did not have a heart.,

You see when I was young.
My parents made me follow rules.
My daddy said this is how the world works
Education is what you need at school.

You see when I was young.
My father told us to obey.
He said don't act up
And that's all my father had to say.
You see when I was a kid.
I was ready to grow.
I use to say I can't wait to be an adult
Boy was I so wrong.

You see when I was little.
I didn't have bills or rent.
I didn't have children to take care of
I had money for me, now I don't have a cent.

It's sad because when I was little.
Rushing to be grown is what I did.
But if I could do it all over again
I wish I could go back to being a kid.

You see when I was a child.
Life was as simple as could be.
All I had to do was play all day.
And my mom cooked and dad took care of me.

My dad used to say stop rushing.
He said you better enjoy being a child
He said you'll grow soon enough.
And you'll regret rushing your childhood after a while.

My First Love

The day that I was born
He laid me in his hands.
He has taken care of me.
And he has always been my man.

He taught me valuable lessons.
And he spoke from his heart.
He loved me unconditionally.
At times when my world fell apart

He showed me how to love people
Just like I loved myself.
He showed me how to give to others.
Even if he had nothing left.

He taught me to be kind.
And let Jesus shine through me.
He said to love people.
And have a kind heart to see

My first love is my Daddy.
My love for him I can't explain.
All that I am and all that I have become
Without him my life would never be the same

My first love is my daddy.
Not once did he ever complain.
The depth of my love for this man
Mere words could never explain.

The Good Samaritan

My dad was a Good Samaritan
To people he gave his all
No matter what they needed.
He always answered his call.

My dad went to work every day
No matter if he was sick or not.
My dad always took care of the home.
And lots of presents on my birthday I got.

My dad was a man of character.
He was not rich, he was really plain
My daddy held his integrity.
Even when he was in a lot of pain.

My dad used to take me to church.
Sometimes I use to use to catch him on his knee
My daddy prayed all the time.
That's when I learned how to pray for me

My daddy use to pick up people
And help them on their way
My daddy always looked out for us.
And still does to this day

My daddy was a Good Samaritan
I owe him more than I could ever repay.
My daddy was my number one supporter
And I took care of him until his dying day.

Did You Know?

Did you know I used to sit there?
And watch you help your friends
Did you know I saw you help others?
When you had time to lend

Did you know I saw you cry?
The day the job laid you off.
Did you know I saw you helped us out?
No matter what the cost

Did you know I was cold outside?
When you had to fix the pipes
Did you know that I saw you be a good husband?
And you never ever griped.

Did you know that I saw your kindness?
When people needed a ride
You gave me money to pay my bills.
And you always stood by my side.

Did you know I saw you go to work?
And you never called in.
You said I have to go pay the electric
And help out a close friend.

Did you know I saw all that?
And no matter what by your kids you did right
You bought us clothes and provided for us
And you never let us go hungry at night

Did you know that I love you?
And you loved me to my worst.
I will forever think the world of you Dad
Because you said I loved you first

I'm Sorry, Daddy

I made a lot of mistakes
Not just one to two
I chose the wrong men
But you stood by me through and through

I've said some things.
That I had no right to say
I was just growing up.
And I was just trying to find my way.

I didn't have all the answers.
And I wasn't trying to rebel.
I was making a series of bad choices
And soon after I fell.

I don't know how to tell you.
How sorry I really am.
I wasn't trying to hurt you.
I was just young please understand.

I know now that you were right.
I should have left that man alone.
Daddy, I'm sorry for not listening.
As I was rushing to become grown

I let you down I know.
I've dealt with my own choices you see
I'm sorry for the choices of my past.
But thank you Daddy for loving me.

I Made It

Dear Daddy, I want to tell you.
I made it see my dream.
I want to tell you daddy.
Thank you for being so mean.

Daddy, I made it.
And I wanted to tell the world.
Daddy you were my backbone.
And I was your little girl

Daddy, I made it.
I live on my own.
Daddy even when I'm not right.
You don't mind saying Baby you wrong.

Daddy, I made it.
I moved out on my own
Even though I wish I could come back to your house
I realize I'm not a kid, I'm grown.

Daddy, I made it.
To see another day
Thanks for holding my hand.
And leading me on my way

Daddy, I made it.
I made it because you loved me so
I'm so glad you are my daddy.
And I just wanted the world to know.

Daddy, I Need You

Daddy, I need you.
My car just broke down.
Daddy, I need you.
Can you come downtown?

Daddy, I need you.
The job just laid me off.
Daddy how can I make it.
I feel like I'm totally lost.

Daddy, I need you.
The bill is due today.
Can you help me?
And you said you were on your way

Daddy, I need you.
My water broke today.
Daddy grabbed the car.
And got me on my way.

Daddy, I need you.
My heart is hurting so bad.
Daddy how will I make it.
When I feel so very sad

Daddy, I need you.
Trouble is everywhere.
You looked up and spoke.
Your burden together we will share.

Daddy, I need you.
I feel like I am going to drown.
You grabbed my hand and said, "Let's pray"
And my faith placed me on solid ground.

Daddy, Why Do You Pray?

Daddy why do you pray?
Each and every night
Daddy why do you ask God.
To make everything alright

Daddy why do you pray?
And go to church all the time
Daddy why do you get on your knees
And say that all will be fine.

Daddy why do you pray?
And say that all is okay.
Daddy, how are we going to make it?
And you say tomorrow will be a better day.

Daddy why do you pray?
When things look bleak
Daddy why do you talk to God.
And his advice for your life you seek.

Daddy why do you pray?
Daddy is God more faithful than man?
Daddy why do you believe in him
Please tell me I don't understand.

Daddy why do you pray?
And you tell us to bow for prayer.
Daddy does prayer help.
Or does it just cause grayer hair?

Daddy why do you pray?
And sometimes life is so unfair.
Daddy why do you say things will look up.
If I just hang in there

Daddy why do you pray?
As I've gotten older, I can say I'm glad you did.
Prayer has been protecting and guiding me.
And taking care of me since I was a kid.

Daddy, I pray now.
And I talk to God every day.
I asked him to order my steps.
And he has never led me astray.

Yesterday

Yesterday my dad was a young man
That could swing me in the air.
That young man
Soon after had a head full of gray hair.

Yesterday my dad worked two jobs.
To take care of my siblings and I
As he got older my dad worked one job.
And wore glasses on his eyes

Yesterday my dad used to drive me around.
And I wish he could today
I wish that I could go pick him up.
Or call and tell him I am on my way.

Yesterday my dad was really healthy
And a lot of medicine he did not take.
As he got older, he got high blood pressure.
And he couldn't eat a seasoned steak

Yesterday my dad carried me in his arms.
And held me in his hand.
Now I carry him in my heart
Because in my eyes he is the greatest man

Yesterday my dad gave me advice.
And told me that life was rough
Now today I face the consequences of choices I made
Even though some were really tough.

Yesterday my dad was a young man.
That was there for me every way.
Now Daddy I'm a successful young woman.
That stops by your grave every day

Daddy's Getting Older

Daddy you are getting older
And it's tearing my heart in two.
I wish that I could rewind the clock
And not ever disobey you.

Daddy, you are getting older.
And you can't do things you use to use to use to do
You always come running when I call.
And I really truly do love you.

Daddy, you are getting older.
And I check on you every day.
I just want to hear your voice.
To make sure that you are okay.

Daddy, you are getting older.
And I don't want you to.
I want you around forever.
Because I don't ever want to lose you

Daddy you are getting older
And you have always been my friend.
No matter when I call.
Time for me you will always lend.

Daddy, you are getting older.
You're not strong as you use to use to be
But if you need strength to stand
You can always lean on me.

Daddy, you are getting older.
And sometimes your vision is not clear.
No matter how old you get I'll be there
Even if in my eyes there are tears.

My Grandfather

The very first person
To hold me in his hand
The very first person
To show me how to be a man

The very first person
To tell me to be still
The very first person
Whose heartbeat I did feel.

The very first person
To give me cereal at night
The very first person that said son,
That is not right.

The very first person that
protects me when mom's mad.
The very first person I call.
When I start to feel really sad

The very first person
That told me to stand tall
My grandfather said life isn't fair.
And sometimes you will fall.

The very first person
To say you need to obey
The very first person that protected me.
When trouble came my way

My grandfather was a simple man.
That loved me with all his might.
No matter what I did in life
He said, "Hold your head up son. It's Alright."

My Father

My father showed me.
The importance of being a friend
My father was there the whole time
From beginning to end

My Role Model

My father was my leader
And he instructed me all the time.
My Father was the reason
I stood straight in line.

My father is intelligent.
I didn't think he was cool.
My father was so strict at times
And he had so many rules

My father was a drill sergeant.
All we did was clean.
We had chores growing up.
And I thought he was so mean.

My father was stern.
All he had to say was no
I walked to my room and accepted it.
When he said with friends I couldn't go

My father was my probation officer.
I always had to check in.
I never had any freedom.
And I could stay out past ten.

My father was tough.
But with me he was always true
He said one day you'll thank me.
For being so hard on you

My father was right.
As I look back on that day
He was wise and I was a fool.
And I miss him dearly every day

One More Day

My friend called me at nine
And said Ava Please come quick.
My daddy is running a fever.
And I think he might be sick.

I said I called 911.
And they said they were on their way.
She said I'm getting dressed.
And I'm calling in to work today.

While on her way to the hospital
I told her to be safe on her way.
I told her not to rush in traffic.
And while driving continue to pray

When I got to the hospital
They rushed him to the ICU.
I asked her what was going on.
And she said Ava I haven't got a clue.

She was shaking all over
And she grabbed my hand real tight.
She said Ava I pray.
That my daddy is alright

We were waiting on the doctor.
And she said everything was just fine
Me and my dad were just up talking.
Now his life is on the line.

She said he was standing.
Then all of a sudden, he fell.
I ran to him as fast as I could
So he wouldn't bump his head on the bed reel

She said Ava I'm so scared.
I said I will stay with you.
She asked if I ever lost my daddy.
I don't know what I should do.

Then I looked down the hall
And I saw the doctor come our way
Everybody got quiet.
Then we heard him sorrowfully say

He said your father is unconscious.
He had an aneurysm in the brain.
My friend got on her knees.
And started calling on Jesus' name.

The doctor said he's not going to make it.
Please contact all your kin
My friend started to break down.
And she started to cry again.

Her family got the news.
And one by one they said goodbye.
My friend looked up and spoke.
Please don't let my daddy die.

She asked me to go into the room with her
As she stood beside his bed
But when she got there she couldn't even talk
She just lay upon him instead.

She grabbed her daddy's hand
And said daddy can you hear.
The preacher told her to stop crying.
Jesus will wipe your every tear.

She said to Ava, "I can't do it.
I can't tell daddy goodbye."
Tears were running down her face
And all she could do was cry.

Her daddy looked like he was sleeping.
As his vitals started to decline
And my friend said my world is shattering.
And I'm going to lose my mind

All of a sudden, he flat lined
and the doctor said I'm sorry he's gone
My friend jumped and stared screaming.
No doctor, you are wrong.

Finally, she sat in the waiting room.
She said I'll never see my dad again
She said to Ava, "I am hurting so bad.
I feel like my life is at its end."

She said I didn't get a chance.
To tell my dad I loved him today.
I'll never get to hug him again.
Or get to hear what he has to say.

One more day to laugh with him.
Another day to see him smile.
One more day to get advice from him.
As I did when I was a child

One more day to ask him.
Am I doing things right?
One more day to thank him.
For being my guiding light

As she went back into the room
Her dad looked peaceful as he lay.
As she stood by the bedside crying
She said Please Jesus, one more day.

Daddy Look

Daddy look I've grown up
I have moved out on my own.
Daddy, I bought me some nice furniture.
And I also live alone.

Daddy looks like I'm responsible.
I have a job that I work every day
I take care of my family.
And I got a raise in the month of May

Daddy, look I did it.
I told you I would make you smile
I have kids that I love with all my heart
And every day we walk a mile.

Daddy, look I went to college.
And I got me a Business Degree
It helped me to obtain a good job.
That has really been a blessing to me.

Daddy look like I'm independent.
I can afford to live on my own.
Thank you for showing me how to be an adult
Daddy look now I'm grown

Another Day

I begin to walk in the building.
Because the funeral started at ten
I passed by all my friends' families.
And so many of her kin

I got to the front of the building
She was seating to my right.
I gave her a big hug
And she grabbed my hand real tight.

She said this is the day.
That I tell my dad goodbye
She grabbed a napkin.
And she begins to cry.

She said I know that he's not hurting
And he is in no more pain.
I called his cell phone last night
Just to hear him call my name.

You know he didn't answer.
He's with Jesus and he's alright.
But knowing that doesn't stop the tears
Or help me sleep at night.

The pastor came in the pulpit.
And service began to start.
My friend said Ava pray for me.
I have so much pain in my heart

As the service was going on
Everybody looked so sad.
My friend asked how you go on.
After you lose your dad?

As she said that I looked down
And I didn't know what to say.
My daddy is still living.
And we were together yesterday.

I said I can't tell you I understand
Or that I know what you are going through
I've never had to endure this.
But I know Jesus can help you.

The thought of me losing my daddy
Would tear my world in two.
I couldn't imagine how she was feeling.
Nor do I ever want to?

I looked at her sorrowfully.
I said Jesus will be there.
Cast all your cares on him.
And I know that for you he cares.

Weeping may endure for a night.
But in the morning the joy will come
She said it feels like I am in a dream
And my body just feels numb.

People got up and spoke.
As the ceremony came to a close
Then the preacher directed the family
And one by one each rose.

When we got in front of the casket
She stood there for a while.
She held her father's hand.
Like she was a little child

She looked at me and said
This is too much for me to bear.
Why did God take my daddy?
You know it's not fair.

My daddy was a good man.
He took care of me.
He would help anybody.
If they asked him, you see.

My daddy was kindhearted.
He always took care of his home.
I need my daddy back.
My Daddy can't be gone.

She said I never thought.
That I would have to go through this
She bent over her father.
And said Good-bye with a kiss.

She said everything that I own Ava.
To the lord I would freely give
If he would give my daddy
Just another day to live.

Father's Day

I got up all excited
It's Father's Day today.
I called my daddy very early.
Just to tell him Hey

I had to stop by the store.
Because I forgot to get him a card
I saw a lady standing by
And she was staring at me hard.

She came over and said hello.
I said how you are.
She said you are so excited.
What are you here to do?

I said It's Father's Day
And I'm on my way to see my dad
I love this holiday.
And she said it makes me real sad.

She said I lost my father.
Today it would make a year.
I am picking flowers.
Then her eyes filled up with tears

She said unlike you I can't see my dad.
And I can't call him on the phone.
I can't tell him to come over.
And ask for his help if something's wrong.

She said I can't tell him happy birthday.
And I can't call him throughout my day.
These flowers are what I gave him.
On his gravestone is where they lay

I wish I could see him again
And I would hug him so tight.
And I'd tell him that I miss him
And I pray for him every night.

Don't take your father for granted.
Listen closely to what I say.
Cherish each moment with him.
Don't just do it on Father's Day

It's Thanksgiving

It's thanksgiving I heard.
At least that's what the calendar said
I don't want to visit my family.
I just want to lay in bed.

This is my first thanksgiving.
Without you here with me
But I've tried not to think about it.
Even when your car I still see.
I hate driving to Vivian.
And you don't come to the door.
No matter how many times I go there
I can't believe I won't see you any more

The turkey is out the oven.
And everyone is standing around.
But then I wait to see you laugh
And I still do not hear a sound.
The dressing is on the table.
But I do not see you with a plate
I look around the room.
and I say Daddy is just late.

You see that is what I tell myself.
In order to keep going on
I had to delete your number.
Because you will never again
Call my phone.
As I stand around with the family
It's just not the same.
No one asks where you are.
But I still call your name.

As we sit around the table
I notice you are not in your chair.
I hold my head down while tears fall
Because to me it still seems unfair

Daddy, Daddy, Daddy
Here is where I want you to be
But on this Thanksgiving, you are with Jesus.
and oh how I wish you were here with me

The Day My Heart Broke

I wake up every day.
With the image I saw that day
I saw you laying in the casket
And I love you is all I can say

You never spoke back.
Because you were not there
You were in heaven with Jesus.
And now you don't have a care.

You don't have to worry.
About bills or issues of this life
You have only happiness.
No more misery or strife

You now walk the streets of glory.
Where angels sing all day long
You happy with the angels
And I pretend that I am strong.

You no longer need medication.
Your blood pressure is ok.
You look young again.
Your hair is no longer grey.

Lord knows that I miss you.
Each and every day
I drive by the graveyard.
Still in disbelief that there you lay.

I see red birds all the time.
And I believe that it is you?
I know it's you checking on me.
To make sure that I'm not blue

I know you saw me.
Stand over the casket that day
My heart was breaking so bad.
Lord help me is all I could say

That day I saw you lying there.
Since that day I've never been the same
How can I ever be normal?
When I have to live with all this pain

Does Time Really Heal?

It has been 11 months and I still cry over my daddy like it was yesterday. I hear people say time heals all wounds and I'm sorry I have to get there first. I do not believe it yet. How does this pain get better? I hear people say that you can survive that kind of loss. I now understand why living life is so hard to do. Eventually you will have to watch all the people you love dearly leave you and go on without you. Time. . . . Give it Time. Time is a tricky thing because time is not promised to any of us. I honestly don't think time will heal the loss of my father. I believe that losing someone is something you never get over . . . . it is something you just survive. I believe that one day everything will make sense but for right now God's will is something I must accept if I call myself a believer.

Give it time people say but what if I don't want to . . . . I just want my father back. Why do I have to get used to living without a man that was my world. However, as far as that question goes I don't know how I will feel years from now all I know is that now I am totally devastated

The Day Before

The day before you died
You called my phone to say.
that you appreciate me for everything
more than words could ever say.

The day before you died.
you got called in to work that night
I never got a chance to see you that day
and knowing that I haven't felt right.

The day before you died.
You seemed happy as can be.
but you had a lot of worries.
and you said baby don't worry about me

You see I was worried about you daddy
but I just knew you would be ok
then I was at the store
and shun called my phone the next day.

The day before you died.
I know Jesus was right there.
He held your hand.
And then he removed all your cares

I Can't Say Goodbye Daddy

That day will forever be considered the worst day of my life. It brings tears to my eyes every time I think of my daddy and any reminders from that day. The clothes that I wore to the funeral I threw away, I have no pictures in my house or on my phone of him till this day. I buried my father 7 years ago and it feels like it was yesterday, the pain of it all still takes the breath out of me. Some days are better than others. One thing I did realize that day is that my life as I knew it was over and this new life ahead was going to have major heartbreak for me as I tried to move forward.

I got up early that morning after lying awake all night. I kept hearing my mother say be strong but I didn't know how to be with him being gone. You see my father was my everything. He was the person in my life that would get my attention like no other. He was my voice of reason and the get up and go that I needed many days for support. I'll never forget getting in the car and it all seemed like a NIGHTMARE. My beautiful FATHER was being laid to rest today. I will never forget driving up to the church and seeing the white hearse. I will never forget seeing people standing all around waiting for the family to go in.

I grabbed boyfriend's hand and I just said Lord please help me to do this. As I approached the building tears fell. I stood there numb not understanding is this for real. Where is my daddy? Why was this happening to me? Tears were all I could see as I approached the altar to see my father's casket. My father's casket are three words that I didn't think that I would be saying this soon in my life. I sat in front of it and I just stared. This just didn't seem real to me. For the life of me I could not comprehend that my father was in this casket.

As the program began, tears started to roll one after the other. My whole body started shaking. Lord, No is all I remember saying I got up to look at my dad over and over again. I'll never forget hearing the preacher say everyone that wants to look, please do so now because once we close the casket you cannot see the body no more. So, I stood up and looked again, I touched his hand and his face. I whispered I love you Daddy for the last time in his ear before I took my seat.

I don't think anything has ever hurt me more in my life than seeing that Funeral Director close the casket on my father's lifeless body. I nearly lost my mind. I was heartbroken and speechless. There are no words that can describe the hurt and pain that still lingers inside of me since that day. I will never forget being a pall-bearer at my father's homegoing.

My sisters and I carried the casket and put it in the hearse. I could not stop looking and I felt like I could not breathe. I got in the car, and I remember my boyfriend saying are you ok, and I nodded yes. . . . However, I was not. Nothing about my life was ok. I felt like my life was over. However, it still did not actually sink in that I was never going to see my dad again.

As we approached the graveyard, I remember walking but slowing down as I got closer. Lord, for this I am not ready. . . . I said over and over again. As I stood by the casket and the grave site. My heart fell to the bottom of my shoes in disbelief that this was taking place. All this time I was still waiting for daddy. Then when the pastor threw dirt on the casket, and everyone started leaving and the casket stayed, and daddy never got out.

That was the moment it hit me. My daddy is gone. . . . At that moment I broke down. The rest of the day was a blur. I saw family and friends and that was a blessing. I'll never forget sitting on my porch and a red bird came and sat on the fence near me. I looked up the meaning of a red bird and it said when you see a red bird that means an angel is nearby. Daddy came to check on me, but it didn't stop me from hurting and missing him.

I'll never forget burying the best man I ever known. I couldn't say goodbye to Daddy, but I did say I'll see you again one day with tears running down my face. He is with Jesus and he's ok now even if I am broken. That is what gives me comfort on the days when it is hard to go on. You never get over losing your father or any loved one. You must go on and know that you will see them again one day. Some days are better than others. The hardest part is learning to live without seeing them in your everyday life. You must pray, remember the good times, and live because that's what they would want. I will love you until my dying day daddy.

www.ingramcontent.com/pod-product-compliance
Lightning Source LLC
Chambersburg PA
CBHW070735030726
47601CB00001B/31